POCKET FACTS

Boats

Philip Steele

M
MACMILLAN

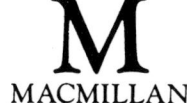

Sail power

People first learned to cross rivers and lakes by floating on tree trunks, bundles of reeds or blown-up animal skins. The oldest surviving remains of a canoe date from about 7000BC. By about 3000BC the Egyptians were building wooden ships with a single, square sail.

galley

Galleys were used in the Mediterranean region. This one was built by the Phoenicians over 2000 years ago. It had a single mast and two banks of oars.

Over the ages, ships were designed to sail further and more easily. Some had extra sails. By 1100 years ago, the Chinese were sailing three-masted ships which were steered by rudders instead of oars. Cogs were European cargo vessels used in the Middle Ages.

cog

Finding the way

The first sailors found their way by looking at the position of the Sun and the stars in the sky. In the Middle Ages sailors learned to measure these positions more accurately. They used various instruments such as those on the right. Compasses were first used in China 2000 years ago. The metal needle always swings northwards.

To the ends of the Earth

European seafarers began to explore the world. In 1492 Christopher Columbus reached the West Indies. Ferdinand Magellan's crew sailed round the world in 1519-21. James Cook (1728-79) explored the Pacific and Southern Oceans.

Captain Cook sailed the *Endeavour* to New Zealand and Australia in 1768-71. In the model (below) you can see the *Endeavour's* lower decks.

Speed and grace

The finest tall sailing ships ever made were known as clippers. They were built during the 19th century for high-speed travel across the world's oceans. American clippers, like the *Pride of Baltimore* (right) were built to carry passengers, cargo and mail. British clippers raced each other to bring back tea from China or wool from Australia. The fastest was the *Cutty Sark*. It once sailed 584 kilometres in a single day.

The stern-wheelers

The first boat to be driven by steam was built in France in 1783. Steam boats with a rear paddle were called stern-wheelers. River steamers played an important part in America. Over 1000 steam boats plied the Mississippi River in the 1830s.

Steaming up the river

This steam boat was called the *Lady Augusta*. It won a prize for racing up Australia's Murray River over 100 years ago. It has paddle wheels on either side.

The giants

The first steamship to sail across the Atlantic Ocean regularly was called the *Great Western*. It was built by the engineer Isambard Kingdom Brunel in 1838. It had sails as well as funnels. Brunel went on to design the *Great Eastern*.

Great Eastern 1858

The golden age of steam

In 1894 a new kind of engine was developed. Steam power was used to drive a set of blades round and round. This 'turbine' was linked to a shaft with a 'screw' or 'propeller' at the end, which pushed the ship forward at high speed. Soon all the passenger liners sailing the Atlantic Ocean were using steam turbines. The *Queen Mary* was one of the fastest, making the crossing in under four days in 1938.

How are modern ships built?

Most large ships afloat today use steam turbines. Modern ships are often huge and very powerful. The largest ships of all are supertankers, built for carrying oil, which can be over 450 metres long. Ships today are often built of huge sections made in a factory. In the shipyard, cranes lift the sections into position, where they are joined together by welding. At the shipyard on the right the ship is already taking shape. The front, or bow, and the rear, or stern, sections are already in position. They are welded to the hull.

How do ships stay afloat?

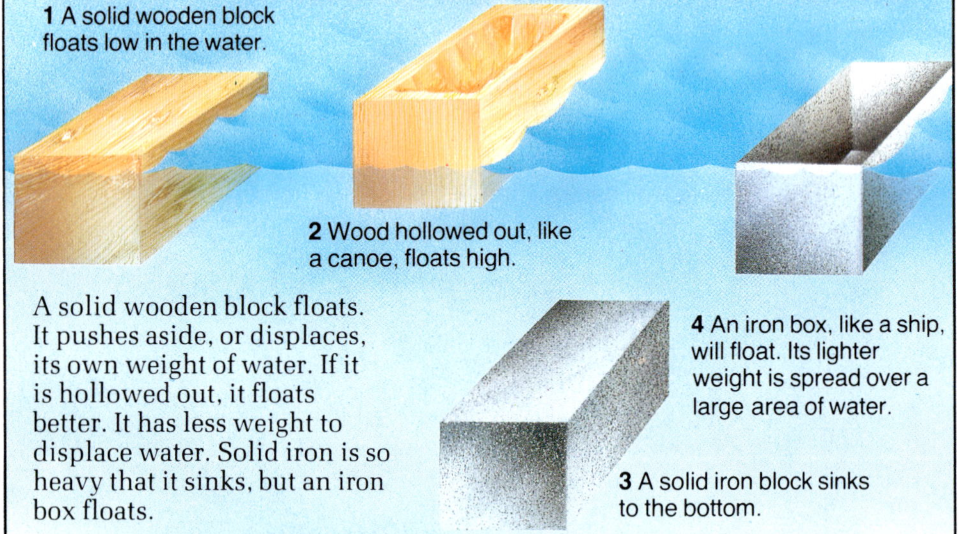

1 A solid wooden block floats low in the water.

2 Wood hollowed out, like a canoe, floats high.

3 A solid iron block sinks to the bottom.

4 An iron box, like a ship, will float. Its lighter weight is spread over a large area of water.

A solid wooden block floats. It pushes aside, or displaces, its own weight of water. If it is hollowed out, it floats better. It has less weight to displace water. Solid iron is so heavy that it sinks, but an iron box floats.

Forward thrust

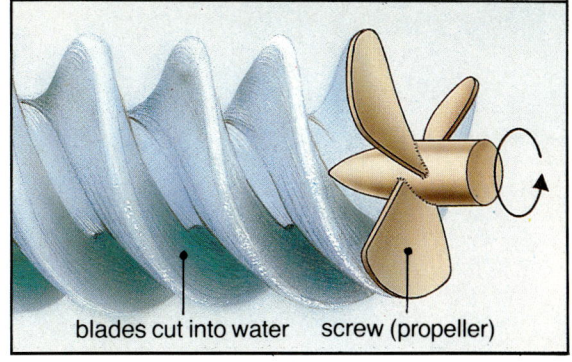

blades cut into water   screw (propeller)

Modern ships are pushed through the water by screws or propellers. These are turned by a shaft linked to the engine or motor. The curved blades of the screw force the water backwards.

How do the ship's turbines work?

In the old days, steam power for the turbine was produced by coal-fired boilers. Today, most large ships use diesel oil to fire their boilers. The steam produced is forced through the turbine at high pressure. The sets of blades inside the turbine are forced to spin at high speed.

Inside a turbine

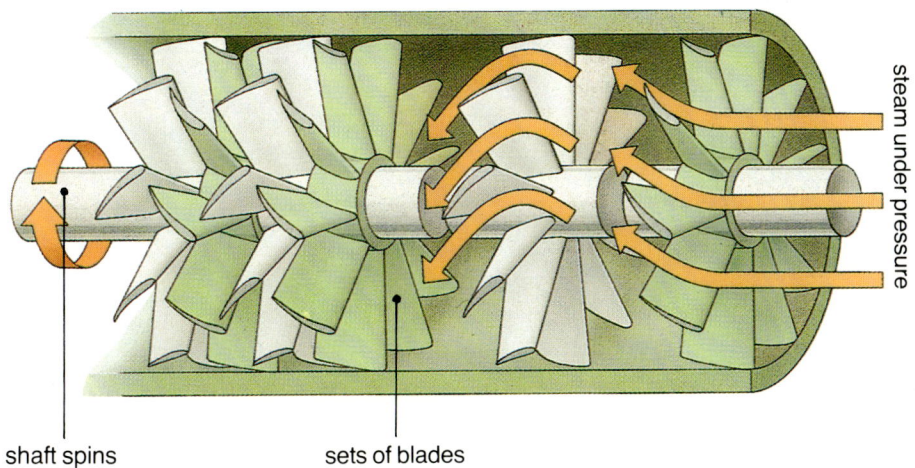

shaft spins   sets of blades

In the first steam turbine ships, the shaft was linked to the propeller by a system of gears. In modern turbo-electric engines, the steam-driven turbine is used to make electricity. This is stored in batteries, which power electric motors. These drive the propellers.

What is sonar?

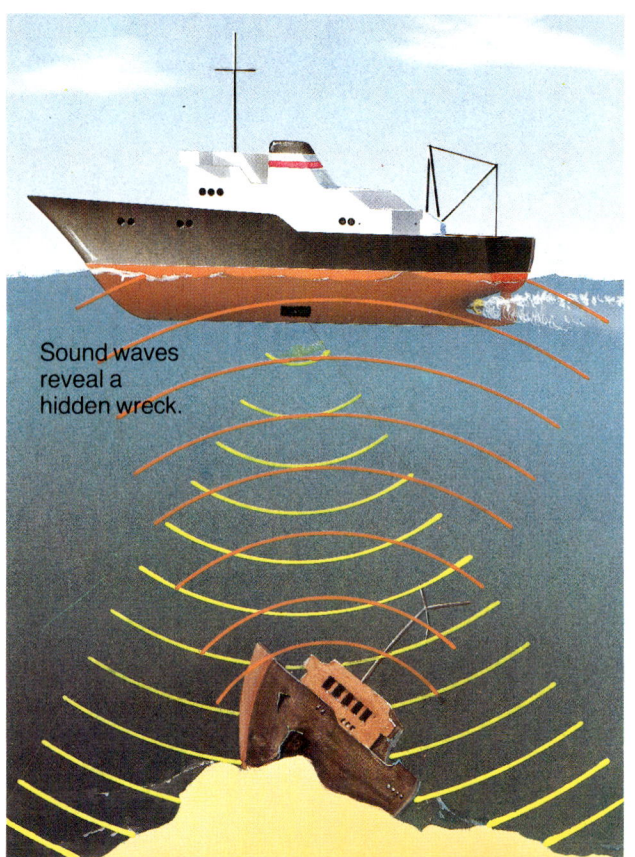

Sound waves reveal a hidden wreck.

Sailors today use many instruments to help them navigate, or find their way at sea.
Sonar stands for **S**ound **N**avigation **R**anging. It is an instrument which sends sound waves through the water. The sounds hit the seabed, or any other object, and bounce back. The echoes are picked up in the ship and timed. They tell the crew how deep the water is beneath the ship. They help the crew know if there are any dangerous reefs or shipwrecks beneath the sea, or submarines. Sonar may also be used by fishing vessels to find shoals of fish.

What is radar?

Radar stands for **Ra**dio **D**etection **A**nd **R**anging. It is an instrument that sends out radio waves in a constantly moving beam. If the beam comes into contact with an object, the beam is bounced back to the ship. There it is picked up and displayed on a screen. Radar warns the crew of approaching shipping or air traffic, or of rocks hidden by fog.

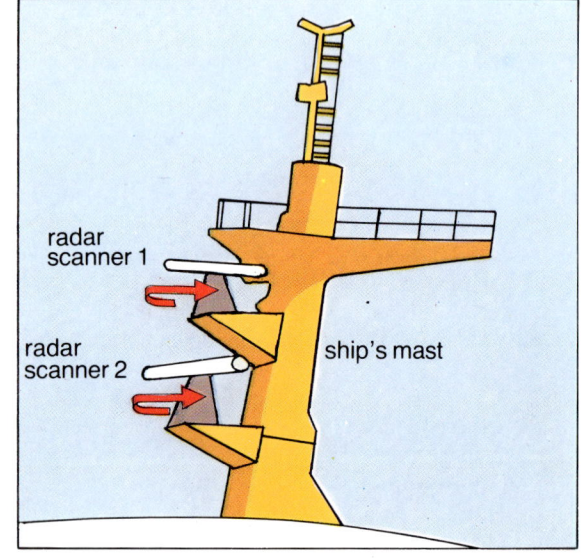

How is radar used?

The ship's officer (right) is looking at a radar screen. A line moves round the screen, showing the direction of the radio waves being sent out. When the radio waves meet another ship or an aircraft, they show up as a small blip on the screen. The officer can tell the exact position and distance, and the ship can change course if necessary.
Radar has helped to improve safety at sea.

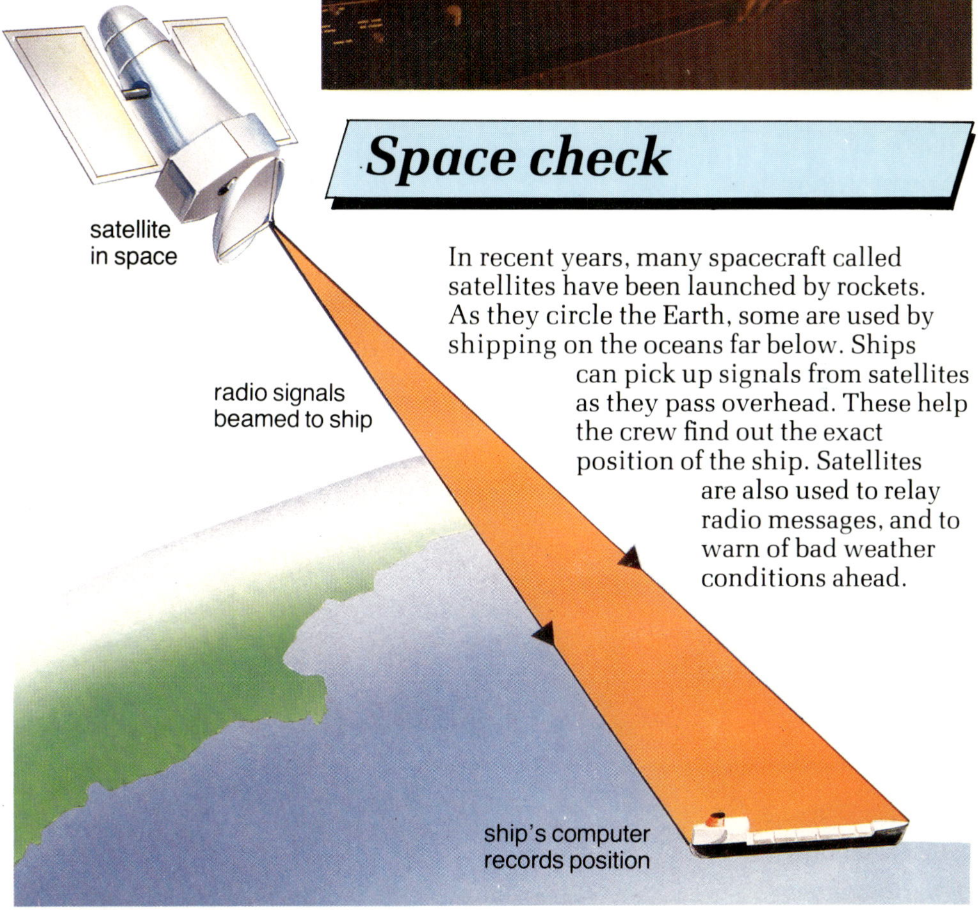

Space check

In recent years, many spacecraft called satellites have been launched by rockets. As they circle the Earth, some are used by shipping on the oceans far below. Ships can pick up signals from satellites as they pass overhead. These help the crew find out the exact position of the ship. Satellites are also used to relay radio messages, and to warn of bad weather conditions ahead.

satellite in space

radio signals beamed to ship

ship's computer records position

Who's in charge?

The wheelhouse of a trawler (left) is full of instruments to help navigation. The skipper is at the wheel, steering the vessel. He is in charge of the ship and its crew.

On a larger ship, the captain has many officers to help run the ship. The raised section of the deck is called the bridge. From here, the captain can use radio to talk to engineers, deck hands, or other crew members.

Keeping in touch

The radio operator (below) has a very important job. Radio is used to keep in touch with other ships and with people on shore. Messages may be taken from harbour authorities or from coastguards. In emergencies, the operator may call for help.

The ship's crew

The cook on this cargo vessel (right) has to cook daily meals for up to 40 crew members. A ship's crew includes all kinds of specialists, from engineers to radio operators. Some keep the ship clean and in good working order. Others may look after the cargo or the passengers.

A hundred years ago, life at sea was very hard. Today ship's crews eat well and have proper cabins to rest in. Voyages may keep the crew at sea for a long time, so it is important that they stay fit and well. Larger ships may have leisure rooms and even on-board swimming pools.

Pilot on board

As the captain brings the ship towards a harbour entrance or a difficult stretch of coast, a small boat may come out to meet the larger vessel. A pilot climbs aboard and is welcomed on to the bridge.

The pilot is someone who knows every detail of the local coastline or harbour. He or she knows each sandbank and hazard, and the marker buoys which act as floating signposts to sailors. The pilot helps the captain steer the ship into port. When ships leave the port, a pilot will be on board once again, to help with navigation. When the vessel reaches the open sea, the pilot will be collected by boat and taken back to shore.

Tug power!

Large ships may need to be towed and turned around in order to dock safely in a busy harbour. Tugs (below left) are tough little boats with very powerful engines. They push the larger vessels or pull them with cables.

Ports and harbours

Ships unload their cargoes in ports or harbours. Rotterdam (below), in the Netherlands, is the world's busiest port. Over 300 large ships can dock there.

Loading ship

Docks are fitted with all kinds of cranes or gantries for loading cargo into the ships' storage sections, or holds. Some goods may be transported loosely, or in boxes or sacks. The goods below are stored in a metal container. Containers have a standard size. They can be transported by road or rail, and are easily stacked. Lines painted on the side of the ship show when it is fully laden.

Container ships

A container vessel (below) sails past Hong Kong Island. Its cargo is contained in large metal boxes, which are stacked neatly on the deck. They are firmly secured in case the weather becomes stormy. A modern cargo vessel can carry up to 1000 containers.

The giant tankers

Tankers (below) are owned by oil companies. Smaller tankers may collect oil from offshore rigs and deliver it to bases or terminals on the coast. Giant tankers carry oil to refineries around the world. They anchor out to sea, and their load is piped ashore.

Ro-ro ferries

Boats that carry people and vehicles over short distances are called ferries. Some boats can only carry vehicles if they hoist them on to the deck with a crane. Other ferries (right) are built with special doors at the bow and stern. These can be raised to allow the vehicles to drive on and off. They are known as Ro-ro ferries, which stands for **Ro**ll on – **ro**ll off. Some can carry 350 cars or 60 trucks. Drivers leave their vehicles on the lower decks, and spend the voyage on the upper decks.

Bulk carriers

Some ships carry loose cargoes which are poured straight into the hold and unloaded by pipes or by mechanical grabs. Such ships are called bulk carriers. At this port in New Zealand (right), wheat is being piped into a bulk carrier. Other loads carried in bulk include coal, sand and iron ore.

Passenger ships

Ships that carry passengers (below) are designed for comfort. The deck space is taken up by comfortable cabins, restaurants, viewing lounges, shops and cinemas. Safety is also important. Note the lifeboats along the side, ready to be lowered at any time. Passengers must know what to do in an emergency.

The QEII

The *Queen Elizabeth II* was launched in 1967. It can carry 2000 passengers in great luxury. It is used for floating holidays, or cruises. The passengers can enjoy a sea voyage with all the comforts of a first-rate hotel. During the cruise they can go ashore to visit interesting sites and buy souvenirs. Some cruise liners travel around the world.

The captain's table

On a cruise ship, there are large numbers of crew members to look after the passengers. The captain must be a perfect host as well as an expert sailor. Below, dinner is being served at the captain's table.

All aboard!

Large ports are always full of small passenger vessels as well as large ones. They may be local ferries or pleasure boats taking tourists on sight-seeing tours. Sometimes cruise liners anchor in mid-harbour, and smaller boats are used to take the passengers ashore.
Hydrofoils (right) are often used as local ferries. They travel at very high speeds. The hull of a hydrofoil is fitted with wing-like structures called foils. These lift the bow out of the water, so that the boat skims over the surface of the waves. The largest hydrofoil ferries can carry up to 250 passengers.

Mayday! Mayday!

When a ship is in danger, it sends out a 'mayday' message (from the French *m'aidez*, 'help me'). Lifeboats and helicopters rush to assist. This lifeboat will not sink even if it is overturned.

To the rescue!

All kinds of special boats are built to help safety at sea. Lifeboat crews and coastguards must be ready to cope with every emergency from fire (right) to sinking vessels and injured sailors. They must be prepared for gales, hurricanes and blizzards. They must know what to do if a ship carrying dangerous chemicals or oil is wrecked. They must keep in touch by radio with air search and rescue teams.

What are lightships?

Some ships are designed to stay in one place, rather than to travel. Lightships are floating lighthouses. They are anchored off sandbanks or reefs as a warning to shipping. The timing of their flashing light helps sailors to recognize their position. They are also equipped with radio, radar, and sound warnings such as foghorns.

Ships at work

Special ships are built to carry out all kinds of jobs at sea. Icebreakers have powerful bows for smashing channels through ice. Dredgers scoop up mud from the sea or river bed. Drilling ships (right) are used by the oil industry. They are floating rigs, used in calm waters to a depth of 1200 metres. The central tower, or derrick, contains the drill-pipe, which bores into the seabed when the ship is in position.

The fishing fleet

The small trawler (below) is fishing for halibut off the North American coast. Trawlers drag huge nets through the sea to catch fish. Some trawlers are very large. They can carry crews of 80 or more and store large catches in their holds.

Harvest of the sea

A single trawl can raise millions of fish. The tiny anchovies (right) are being piped on board from the net. Modern fishing methods have led to over-fishing in some areas. If too many young fish are caught, there will be fewer left to breed. Catches must be strictly controlled by international agreement.

Coastal fishing

Not all seafood is gathered by large fishing fleets. All around the world single small boats fish coastal waters. They catch crabs, lobsters, shrimps and prawns, octopuses and small fish. The Irish fishermen (right) are lowering lobster pots into the water. They will mark the position of the pots with floats and return later to collect their catch.

Catch for sale

The fishermen at this port in Thailand (left) pack their catch with ice to keep it fresh. Large trawlers have refrigerated storage to keep the fish in good condition.
In some places, the catch is sold directly to the public on the beach or dockside. In others, the fish is sold off to dealers at a market. They sell it to fish shops or to factories for processing. Fish is an important source of food for a hungry world.
The fishing fleet does important work, but life on a trawler can be very hard. It is often wet and bitterly cold. The trawler may be battered by storms and high waves. The work can be tiring and dangerous.

Clearing a way

Much of the world's shipping uses inland waterways, such as lakes, rivers and canals. Rivers such as the Nile, the Rhine, the Yangzi and the Ganges are ancient trading routes, and are still busy today. Some rivers are deep and can take very large ships. Others are shallower. River boats may need to be flat-bottomed, so that they can travel through these shallows. Rivers and canals may carry a lot of mud or silt in their waters. This can build up on the riverbed until boats are unable to travel upstream. Dredgers (left) must be used to dig out this silt.

Deep-water canals

The longest single canal open to ocean-going vessels is the Suez Canal (below). It is 162 kilometres long, and links the Mediterranean with the Red Sea. It was built between 1859 and 1869. Before it was opened, ships sailing from Europe to India had to sail round southern Africa.

Locks and engines

The 68 kilometre-long Panama Canal (left) links the Atlantic and Pacific Oceans. Note the electric engines on rails, which tow ships through the locks. Locks are like steps built into canals. They allow boats to move from one level to another. The water level inside a sealed section of the canal is raised or lowered, so that the ship can move forwards.

Working barges

Most rivers and canals are not deep enough to carry ocean-going vessels. Goods are carried instead of flat-bottomed barges (left). Several barges may be lashed together and pushed by a single vessel.

River boats

In parts of South America, Africa and Asia, there are few roads and railways. Most passengers and goods are carried by river boats. On the Tapagos River (left) goods are brought to market by water.

Into the unknown

Small, simply built boats are as important today as they have always been. The expedition (below) is making its way through the South American rain forest. The easiest way through the thick jungle is to follow the course of a river in a small wooden boat. Boats have always been used for exploring remote regions. Canoes, dinghies, rafts and small boats of all shapes and sizes are in everyday use all over the world. They can be made of wood, animal skins, rubber, fibreglass, metal or plastic.

Messing about in boats

Even if people do not use boats for work or transport, they often enjoy owning or renting a boat just for fun.
Narrowboats and barges (left) were once used to carry goods on canals in Britain. They were often pulled along by horses on the towpath. Today, they are used by holiday makers. After driving on a motorway or a city street, nothing could be more peaceful than floating gently along the old waterways. The boats are often restored and painted in bright colours. Some people live on them.

Boats for living in

Boats are used as homes in many parts of the world. The traditional houseboat (below) is on a lake in Kashmir, to the north of India. Houseboats are common in many Asian countries and in some European cities, such as Amsterdam.

Boating for pleasure

A spinnaker sail (right), like a great balloon, drives a sailing boat through the water. Sailing is one of the most popular sports of all. Pleasure boats range from small sailing dinghies to luxury yachts. Famous races include the America's Cup, the Admiral's Cup and the Round-the-World Race. Yacht design has produced many new types of boat, such as the two-hulled catamaran and the three-hulled trimaran. Yachts are divided into different classes for racing.

Motor boats and high-speed powerboats are also popular and compete in races at speeds of up to 166 kph. Rivers offer their own challenges, with canoeing and white-water rafting.

The dhow

The dhow (below) is a kind of sailing boat seen in the Indian Ocean and Arabian Sea. Its wooden hull (left) is powered forward by a swooping sail called a lateen. Its classic shape has influenced ship design over the ages.

The dugout

The dugout canoe was probably the first kind of boat ever made. It is hollowed out from a single tree trunk. It is still in use in many parts of the world. The herders (below) are crossing a river in Botswana.

The kayak

The kayak (below) is a graceful canoe used by the Inuit or Eskimoes of the Arctic. It is made of seal skins stretched over a frame of wood or bone.

The sampan

The word sampan comes from the Chinese *san pan*, which means 'three boards'. The term is used to describe any of the small boats used around the rivers and coasts of China and South East Asia. They are powered by a single oar at the stern. They are often roofed over with matting. The boats below were photographed on a river in Thailand. Many people live in small boats like the one on the left.

The record-breakers

Turbinia 1894

★ The biggest ship ever built was an oil tanker called the *Seawise Giant*. It was launched in 1976 and had a length of 458 metres. It was destroyed in 1988.

★ The first vessel to use steam turbines was built by Charles Parsons in 1894. It was called the *Turbinia* and could travel at 64 kph. The 30-metre long ship had three turbines. Its appearance at a naval review in 1897 impressed many ship designers. They ordered new, large ships to be built with steam turbines.

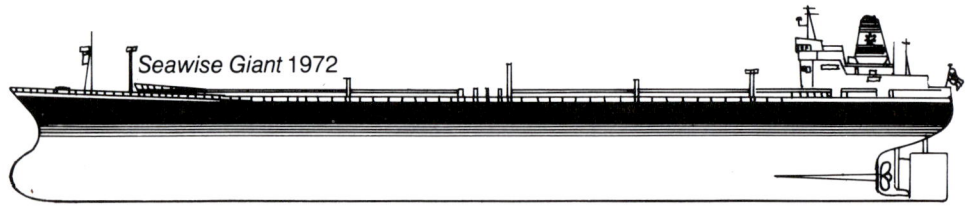

Seawise Giant 1972

★ The water speed record is held by the hydroplane *Spirit of Australia*. Driven by Kenneth Warby, it crossed an Australian reservoir at over 511 kph in 1977.

★ The fastest propeller boat on record is the *Texas*, which in 1982 reached 369 kph in California, in the United States. It was driven by Eddie Hill.

★ The first man to sail solo non-stop around the world was Robin Knox Johnston, in *Suhaili*, in 1968-9. It took him 312 days. The first woman to do this was Kay Cottee in *First Lady*, in 1987-8.

★ The first people to row across the Pacific Ocean were John Fairfax and Sylvia Cook in *Britannia II*, in 1971-2. It took 362 days. The first to row across the Atlantic, in 1897, were George Harboe and Frank Samuelsen in *Fox*. It took 55 days.

★ The fastest crossing of the Atlantic by sail was in 1988. Serge Madec's *Jet Services 5* travelled from the United States to Cornwall in England in 7 days, 6.5 hours. The fastest powerboat to cross the Atlantic was Richard Branson's *Virgin Atlantic Challenger II*. In 1986 it made the crossing in 3 days 8.5 hours.

★ The heaviest passenger ship in the world is the *Sovereign of the Seas*, a Norwegian cruiser weighing over 73 000 tonnes. The longest is the *Norway* (formerly *France*) which is 316 metres from bow to stern.

★ The largest Ro-ro ships are in service off Florida in the United States. They are 177 metres in length, weigh 16 700 tonnes, and can carry over 375 loaded trucks.

★ The biggest shipbuilder in 1987 was Hyundai of Korea.

★ The largest sailing vessel ever built was the *France II*. Launched in 1911, the ship was nearly 128 metres long.

France II 1911

Index

The numbers in **bold** are illustrations

barges 2, 23, **23**, 24, **24**,
Branson, Richard 29
bridge 10, 11
Brunel, Isambard Kingdom 5
bulk carriers 15, **15**

canals 22, 23
  Panama 23, **23**
  Suez 22, **22**
canoes 2, 24, 25
  dugout 26, **26**
  kayak 27, **27**
cargo vessels 2, 11
Chinese 2
clippers 3, **3**
coastguards 10, 18
Columbus, Christopher 3
compasses 2, **2**
container ships 14, **14**
containers 12, 14
Cook, James 3
Cook, Sylvia 29

dhows 26, **26**
dinghies 25
docks 13, **13**
dredgers 19, 22, **22**
drilling ships 19, **19**

Endeavour 3, **3**
Egyptians 2

Fairfax, John 29
ferries 17
fishing 20-1
France II 29, **29**
fuels 7
funnels 5

galleys 2, **2**

Harboe, George 29
Hill, Eddie 29
houseboats 25, **25**
hydrofoils 17, **17**
Hyundai 29

icebreakers 19
inland waterways 22-3

Jet Services 5, 29

Knox Johnston, Robin 29

lifeboats 16, 18, **18**
lightships 19, **19**
locks 23, **23**

Madec, Serge 29
Magellan, Ferdinand 3
marker buoys 11, **11**
masts 2
mayday messages 18
motor boats 25

narrowboats 24
navigating 2, 8, 11

oars 2
over-fishing 20

Parsons, Charles 28
passenger liners 5, 16-17, **16**
  Norway 29
  Queen Elizabeth II 16, **16**
  Queen Mary 5, **5**
  Sovereign Seas 29
Phoenicians 2
piloting 11
pleasure boats 17, 25
ports 12
powerboats 25
Pride of Baltimore 3, **3**
propellers (screws) 12

races 3, 25
radar 8, **8**, 9, **9**
radio 10, **10**, 18
rafts 24, 25
river boats 23, **23**
Ro-ro ferries 15, **15**, 29
rudders 2

sails 5
  lateen 26
  spinnakers 25, **25**
sampans 27, **27**

Samuelsen, Frank 29
satellites 9, **9**
shipbuilding 6, **6**
sonar 8, **8**
Spirit of Australia 29
steam boats 4-5
  Great Eastern **5**
  Great Western 5
  Lady Augusta 4
steam power 5, 7
steam turbines 5, 6, 7, 28
  Turbinia 28, **28**
stern-wheelers 4, **4**
submarines 8
supertankers 6, **6**, 14, **14**

Texas 29
trawlers 10, **10**, 20-1, **20**
tugs 12, **12**

Virgin Atlantic Challenger II 29

wheelhouse 10, **10**

yachts 25
  catamarans 25
  trimarans 25

© Macmillan Publishers Limited 1989

All rights reserved. No reproduction, copy or transmission of this publication may be made without written permission.

No paragraph of this publication may be reproduced, copied or transmitted save with written permission or in accordance with the provision of the Copyright Act 1956 (as amended), or under the terms of any licence permitting limited copying issued by the Copyright Licensing Agency, 33-4 Alfred Place, London WC1E 7DP.

Any person who does any unauthorised act in relation to this publication may be liable to criminal prosecution and civil claims for damages.

First published 1989

Published by Macmillan Children's Books
A division of MACMILLAN PUBLISHERS LTD
Houndmills, Basingstoke, Hampshire RG21 2XS
and London
Companies and representatives
throughout the world

Design by Julian Holland Publishing Ltd
Cover concept by Groom and Pickerill

Printed in Hong Kong

British Library Cataloguing in Publication Data

Steele, Philip
Boats
1. Boats & ships – For children
I. Title II. Series
623.8'3

ISBN 0 333 51458 0

Acknowledgements
Illustrations: BLA Publishing Ltd, Nigel White;
Photographs: *a = above, m = middle, b = below*
2*b*, 3*a*, National Maritime Museum, London; 3*b*, 4*a*, ZEFA; 5*b* University of Liverpool; 6*a* ZEFA; 9*a* Racal-Decca Company; 10*a* Alex Williams/Seaphot; 10*b*, 11*a* Overseas Containers Ltd; 11*b* T&D Crossley/Seaphot; 12*a*, 12*b*, 13 ZEFA; 14*a* Susan Griggs Agency; 14*b* British Petroleum; 15*a* ZEFA; 15*b* Barnaby's Picture Library; 16*a* ZEFA; 16*b* British Caledonian; 17*a* P&O Cruises Ltd; 17*b* Boeing Company; 18*a* Royal National Lifeboat Institute; 18*b* ZEFA; 19*a*, 19*b* Barnaby's Picture Library; 20*a* Susan Griggs Agency; 20*b* South American Pictures; 21*a* T&D Crossley/Seaphot; 21*b* ZEFA; 22*a* Ivor Edmonds/Seaphot; 22*b*, 23*a*, 23*m* ZEFA; 23*b* South American Pictures; 24*a* The Hutchinson Library; 24*b* Chris Fairclough; 25*a* The Hutchinson Library; 25*b* Yachting World; 26*a left*, 26*a right* ZEFA; 26*b* Peter Johnson/NHPA; 27*a* John Lythgoe/Seaphot; 27*b* Douglas Dickins